Fatherhood, Football, Turning & Forty

Fatherhood, Football, & Turning Forty

Chris Crowe

Bookcraft
Salt Lake City, Utah

Library of Congress Catalog Card Number: 95-76157
ISBN 0-88494-989-3

First Printing, 1995

Printed in the United States of America

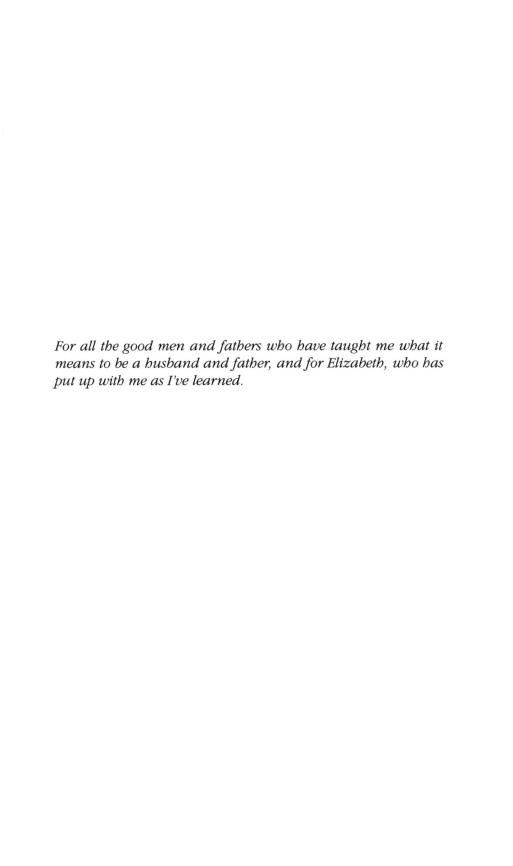

For all the good men and fathers who have taught me what it means to be a husband and father, and for Elizabeth, who has put up with me as I've learned.

Contents

Disclaimer

I am not a General Authority, nor am I related to or intimately acquainted with one. (But I did shake hands with President Kimball on two separate occasions.) I am not a bishop or former bishop. I did not serve a mission, and I don't have any pioneer heritage. I have no professional sports background; I've never made or starred in a movie, written or recorded a song, won any awards, secured a patent, invented something, or published a best-seller. Likewise I am not a motivational expert, a counselor, an Eagle Scout, a millionaire, a surgeon, a lawyer, a dentist, a carpet layer, interior designer, plumber, or anyone else you might want to seek out for serious advice.

I'm just a father to four children and a husband to Elizabeth, and I teach Gospel Doctrine and try, but haven't yet managed, to get 100 percent home teaching regularly.

That does not mean that I don't like talking about myself. I *love* telling other people what I've done and what I think, but I know most of it is merely pleasant diversion, a little friendly hot air.

Anyway, you're welcome to read on. But don't get your hopes up.

The Triple Threat:
Priesthood, Husbandhood,
Fatherhood

I'd been a member of the Church a scant twelve months and twenty-six days when Liz and I married, hardly enough time to get much serious gospel study done. And being preoccupied, as I was, with college classes, marriage preparations, and the growing pressure of showing affection to my fiancée in ways that wouldn't lead to trouble, I'd learned barely enough to earn a temple recommend.

After more than two decades, my understanding of the gospel has increased, but I still feel stupid, even illiterate, in many gospel and scriptural conversations. I haven't memorized any scriptures. I don't have seminary or mission stories to tell. And, maybe because of my gentile background, I've never really been interested in gospel mysteries and Church politics, topics that seemingly occupy the thoughts and conversations of many. I do try to read the *Ensign* and the scriptures, to stay awake in sacrament meeting and general conference, and to prepare for my Sunday School class. That has helped, but my knowledge of the Church and gospel remains pretty basic and practical.

In the last twenty years, though, I have learned a lot about being a Mormon male, and, believe me, it's no picnic. Married

Mormon men are perpetually prodded by a trident, the three-pronged dilemma of responsibilities: priesthood, husband-hood, and fatherhood. In lesson manuals and sacrament talks, these three never conflict, rarely overwhelm, but in real life we all know they can leave us feeling as helpless and hung up as a gigged frog.

Shortly after I got married, I learned about the tripartite duties in a priesthood meeting of the BYU 87th Branch in the basement of one of the buildings of Wymount Terrace, the married student housing at BYU. Our branch president was James Killian, a local seminary teacher and father to more children than I could conceive of at the time, a man who understood very well what a branch full of new husbands and fathers needed to learn. So one Sunday morning, he taught us that we were patriarchs, at least patriarchs of our own homes. As such, we were responsible for our own temporal and spiritual welfare, that of our wives, and, when the time came, that of our children. No problem, my newly wed self thought. I can do that. Easy.

And it was easy at first. The honeymoon afterglow combined with an unfettered simple life without children to build a false sense of complacency, an overconfidence. But in time you learn it's a heavy calling, and it never seems to get easier. At first, you just have to worry about yourself and your wife. Pretty soon, you add a baby, then another, and another, and another (and for some men, many, many others). These kids need food and clothing and discipline and money and training and help with homework and driving lessons and chaperoning and talks about sex and encouragement and support and spankings and friends and merit badges and priesthood blessings and hobbies and vacations and medicine and toys and beds and blankets and books and magazines and And ANd AND. . . Children become a kind of reverse cornucopia, perpetually sucking up all the material and emotional resources of their parents.

And you're constantly nagged by the fear that you're not doing this priesthood-husbandhood-fatherhood thing right, that your stupidity and foibles are ruining your kids. When you have teenagers, this fear increases, in part because they regularly point out your foibles and stupidity. The insecurity gets worse when you're around families whose kids seem, compared to yours, practically perfect in every way. You pray to God for inspiration on how to raise them, how to help them, how to be a righteous parent, but the answers come slowly, obscurely, no brighter than the dim and shaky beam of the flashlight you keep forgetting to buy new batteries for. No matter what you do, no matter how good your intentions are, the kids continue to grow up, imperfect and human. You know, of course, that their imperfections are not your fault, that the little agonies they endure in school and in adolescent society are unavoidable and necessary, and that these creatures who were once helpless but perfect babes and later became the six- , seven- , and eight-year-olds with iron-clad testimonies of your infallibility now question your common sense regularly. Yet you remain hopeful, prayerful that when the hormones raging in their arteries subside in seven or eight years, they'll still be on the right path, happy and successful. Coping with all this as a father is more difficult than trying to kiss your thirteen-year-old son on the cheek in public.

The responsibilities don't end with children. Once you've got a child or two, additional church responsibilities start coming your way. A little home teaching at first, then you're thrown to the Boy Scouts or the Young Men program and the discretionary hours fly away like a pack of ravenous deacons to a buffet table. The elders quorum waits to nab you as soon as you're turned loose by the youth programs, and after that, well, stake missions, Sunday School, Primary, Cub Scouts, the activities committee, bishoprics, and, for an unlucky few, the big B-job: Bishop. You don't mind these callings, because you recognize and appreciate the blessings such service brings, but they're an added and distracting burden to your other duties.

Committed as you are to your church duties, you smack head on into the first of the married Mormon male conflicts. Do you spend a jillion hours a week with the teachers quorum and Varsity Scouts, or do you stay home evenings to read with your kids and play a little basketball with them after dinner? Do you go on camp outs every month and leave your wife alone with the kids, again and again? Do you spend your one and only precious week of summer vacation chaperoning girls' camp instead of taking your family on a trip to visit grandparents? And if you do choose to spend time with your kids instead of your church calling, how do you handle the inevitable guilt that follows? When you miss weeknight church meetings to watch your daughters play soccer, are you a worthless slouch in the eyes of the bishop? Of the Lord?

Of course you know that the key is balance, that it's not one without the other but both together. Planning helps. So does a good attitude. And often you strike that happy balance and life seems good. But inevitably times come when you must choose the lady or the tiger, and, regardless of what you choose, you're gobbled up by guilt and regret: "Really shoulda gone to that meeting." "Wish I'd been at my son's game." You want to do what's right, what's best, but when faced with two right choices, you sometimes feel like you're wrong no matter what you choose.

The third prong of this trident of married Mormon male duties is husbandhood. You know you and your wife are supposed to get through life together as happily and righteously and permanently as possible and that you're supposed to regularly cultivate your relationship. And you want to: that's why you got married in the first place. But the kids pull one way, the job another, the church callings yet another. You're drawn and quartered, pulled in four different directions by four important, righteous responsibilities. You yearn for those simple honeymoon days when nothing but your wife mattered.

She still matters, more than ever, but so do the kids, the church callings, the job. You do your best to find time to talk with her, to be alone together, to give her time for herself, but you're not very good at it. In this male society, you feel the pressure to provide for the family, to work at the office and at church, and to leave the kids and home things to her. Besides, she's good at it, has more patience with the kids than you ever will, can get house jobs done in half the time you can. She supports and encourages you to do well, to do what's right, so off you go, happy and relieved. But in your clearer moments you wonder if it's fair. Is it right for her to be saddled with all the housework? Aren't the kids yours as much as hers?

Wouldn't she find activities outside the home as fulfilling and rewarding as you do?

But if she does, more of the burden of home and kids falls on your shoulders. And stretched as you already are, can you handle it? Do you want to handle it? It is often an incredible luxury to say good-bye in the morning and lose yourself in the world of work for eight or ten hours and then return home after most of the daily battles have been waged and won. You're tired at the end of the day, and it's nice—very, very nice—to have someone make your dinner, clean your clothes and house, and care for your kids while you're away. But you know, deep inside, that you could do it; it would be a huge sacrifice, but you could do it: share things; lighten her load; be a better husband, a better, truer helpmeet.

For a while, you try it. You get better. But a crisis at work or a new church calling pulls you away and everything falls back to her. You know that it's hard on her, that she's worn out, and you feel guilty, inadequate. Once again, you're torn by the three married Mormon male responsibilities.

Some men juggle priesthood, husbandhood, and fatherhood with ease, but most of us, I think, fumble one or two fairly often. But we stay at it, working to keep all three moving, and when the rhythm's right and the motion's fluid and everything's clicking, there's no better feeling in the world. However, in my weaker moments when I'm overwhelmed and pierced and bleeding by the trident, I sometimes yearn for my former, simple, single life—no kids, no wife, no church responsibilities. Ahh, then I could really focus my efforts, I think to myself, I could really get some serious things done.

I realize such thoughts are only temporary insanity. Life would be too empty, too lonely, too selfish without the trident, without the duties and *pleasures* of priesthood, husbandhood, and fatherhood. It is not an easy life, but having lived it this far and having tasted the bitter and the sweet fruit that it yields, I would choose no other: it has shaped me, is shaping me, into the kind of man I want to be.

I See the Tumor,
She Sees the Gas

It recently occurred to me that we're all terminal cases. We know our time in the game is limited, but we don't know when the final buzzer will sound. That's partly what makes it all interesting, I guess. Maybe that's why middle-aged men are so preoccupied with death, or at least why *I* am so preoccupied with death. And the Church doesn't help at all, with all its talk about the dead: our dead ancestors, recent funerals, things we need to do to endure to the End (implying that there are things some of us won't get done before the End), even the Dead Sea Scrolls.

Whatever the reason, It, my death, is almost always on my mind, probably nestled just behind the little inert chunk of brain cells that could, at any moment, turn malignant on me. I realize I could go anytime due to a car wreck, a bolt of lightning, a slimy chunk of artery-blocking cholesterol. I'm not morbid about It; I just want to be prepared. It's a middle-aged male thing.

Last week, for example, thinking about It, I decided I'd better remind Liz how to use my life insurance death benefit. Just in case.

"Pay off the mortgage first thing. That will leave you a couple hundred thousand. Then invest the rest in something safe and see, in the first year, if the interest will be enough to live on. Without a house payment and with almost no taxes, you could probably make it okay. Unless J.C.'s on his mission by then.

"And you might want to look into buying a condo as a rental property, but that'd mean you'd have to manage it, and you may not have the time or expertise—"

She pointed out that I wasn't even sick.

That didn't stop me. I finished my financial overview and reminded her of The Letter in her desk.

The Letter came as a result of my closer-than-I-cared-for brushes with the end of the Fourth Quarter. Neither was pleasant, but each reminded me that I don't have all the time in the world to take care of business and that I'm fortunate to be playing in an overtime period.

Four years ago, a few more aches and pains than normal sent me to my family doctor for what I figured would be a routine exam that would lead to a prescription or two, a lecture about my weight and diet, and a reminder to have my Norwegian moles examined annually. Unfortunately, it didn't go as planned. The doctor poked me, examined my various orifices, drew enough blood to float a Cadillac, and then, so casually that I almost didn't get it, said, "Maybe you ought to go see a specialist."

His nurse made the appointment.

Dr. A breezed into the examination room, chatted for a few minutes about the weather, life in general, the medical history of my parents, and began his exam: listened to my heart, thumped my back, poked my abdomen, then looked at my legs. He squeezed one shin, then the other. He did it again and whistled. "You've got ten or fifteen pounds of fluid in there."

So?

"Looks like possible heart failure. How long have you had these symptoms?"

Heart failure? Whoa, start my heart up, will you? I thought heart failure meant the old pump had quit. Was I dead or dying on the examining table?

That exam led to a diuretic prescription that kept me within sprinting distance of restrooms for the next three months. It also led to vascular exams, X-rays, and other kinds of unpleasant heart examinations I have chosen not to remember.

But it also led to my early awakening the very next morning—the first morning of the rest of my life, at least what was left of my ever-shortening mortal probation. At the desk in our bedroom, with the ocean breeze blowing over me, I did the kind of thing middle-aged men do when they're contemplating their imminent demise: I composed The Letter, detailing to my wife the various and sundry assets we owned, the phone number to our life insurance company, the account number of my retirement plan, my social security number, the addresses of property we owned, including our grave sites. I then outlined the program for my funeral: speakers, music, pallbearers, and expressed my eternal love for her and our children. A very sad and very depressing letter.

I shed a few tears of regret at my untimely passing, looked in on the still slumbering kids, sighed wistfully, then went back to the desk and addressed the envelope, "To Be Opened in the Event of My Death," and placed it in my wife's desk drawer.

Fortunately, she hasn't had to read it yet.

But that was only the beginning. When Dr. A was finished with me, he referred me to Dr. B.

Sitting in Dr. B's waiting room, I noticed that I was distinctly unlike most of my fellow patients: I still had a full head of hair. Everyone else, and most tried to hide it beneath scarves or baseball caps, had thin, stringy hair; some had none at all. So I've got alopecia. The doc is trying to head off male-pattern baldness. It was a symptom I hadn't noticed, but I trusted my family doctor. I wouldn't have guessed he'd send me to a cancer specialist.

My name was called. I shuffled behind the nurse to my examination room.

Dr. B strode in, all business. "Chris, we're going to do a series of tests. We're not sure, but you may have some form of intestinal cancer."

His prostate exam was no less direct.

By the time I caught my breath, he had finished with me

and was mapping out a series of little indignities, the kinds of probing and poking and pricking and questioning that men over age forty gradually learn to live with. That was merely a warm-up for the real indignities that would soon follow: a barium enema, a twenty-four-hour urine sample (try explaining to your kids why you carry a gallon tank into the bathroom), CAT scans, and some extremely unpleasant biopsies.

Through it all, in addition to hoping the tests would turn up negative (or positive, depending on your point of view), I kept reminding Liz of The Letter in her desk, calculating my life insurance benefit and the amount of interest it would earn annually, and feeling pretty miserable about leaving my kids and wife before I was good and ready to. Though sympathetic to my gloom, Liz kept reminding me of her confidence that I'd live.

Well, she was right, I lived, but my terminal experiences and my inexorably advancing age have only deepened my morbidity. Not that long ago, I had extreme difficulty understanding why newspapers published obituaries. Now I read them looking for deceased who are younger than I am. Now I read, and am interested in, articles about the prostate, a dumb little organ I didn't even know existed two or three years ago. And I worry—worry about cholesterol, salt, and fat; about secondhand smoke and ultraviolet rays; about drunk drivers and gun-toting lunatics; about life insurance and mortgages; about the kids and college and missions and marriages. And, of course, I worry that I worry too much.

It's made me into something of a pessimist, though I hardly think of myself that way. But an experience this morning, another middle-aged indignity, made it pretty clear that when it comes to my health, I tend to see the glass as half-empty.

It was an IVP, an intravenous pyelograph, a surprisingly painless dye and X-ray kind of thing. But it has an ominous purpose: identifying little nuggets of junk that might be clogging important organs or tracts, marking organs that are inflamed or flabby, diagnosing malignant things inside. When the test was nearly finished, I was told to use the restroom before the final series of X-rays. On my way to the restroom, I passed through the X-ray reading room and saw my kidneys up on the light board. I immediately wished I hadn't. There, in the lower right-hand corner of each X-ray, appeared a sinister dark spot.

My knees weakened and my hands turned cold.

When I climbed back up on the X-ray table, Liz, who, kind and supportive wife that she is, had stayed at my side through this most recent trial, asked me why I looked so pale.

"I saw my X-rays," I said. "There's a dark spot on the bladder or kidney or something. It doesn't look good."

Her eyes widened and she bit her lip. We were both scared more than before, but she assured me it was probably nothing. I appreciated her optimism but was certain I'd just seen my tumor. *My* optimism hoped it would turn out to be benign.

When the exam was over, the technician came in and announced that no kidney stones had shown up, no abnormal organs were revealed, no blockages discovered. Everything looked clear and normal. It had merely been an infection.

Yeah, right. He's just letting my doctor tell me about the tumor. Professional courtesy.

After I had changed back into my clothes, I found Liz in the X-ray reading room looking at my X-rays with the technician. He was pointing out this and that, where the dye had been and what it revealed.

Then she asked about the ominous dark spot.

"Oh, that?" he said, tapping my tumor with his index finger. "That's just gas."

Ceremonies of Separation

My fifteen-year-old daughter, Christy, has not called. She's been gone now for five days and five nights, and we've not heard a single word from her. When she left for a week's worth of Especially for Youth at BYU, I pressed a quarter into her palm. "Call us tonight," I said. "Let us know how you're doing."

I assume she's doing okay; I *hope* she's doing okay. I'm pretty sure she's doing okay, because the hospital and the police haven't called, nor have any EFY officials. I think what has really bothered me the most, though, isn't the fact that she hasn't called—it's that she hasn't *needed* to call. She's too busy or having too much fun (probably both). Still, she *should* call. I'm her father and I want to know how she's doing. She probably thinks, though, that I want to intrude, to check up on her, to dampen her fun. I don't. I just want to be needed, to be connected, to feel like a father. For all of her fifteen years and nineteen days on this planet, I have been her father, and she has needed me for food or comfort or clothing or money or a ride or something—always something. But this week has given me a glimpse into what my life will be like without her, when she no longer depends on me, no longer needs me.

I don't like the feeling.

It's not my first encounter with pre-empty nest syndrome. I remember when I walked Jonathan to his first day in American school. We had lived in Japan for three years, and he had attended preschool and first and second grade in Japanese schools. We then moved to Hawaii, and one August morning I walked Jonathan from our house on Kulanui Street to his classroom at Laie Elementary School. He was understandably anxious about being a new kid in school, about attending, for the first time in his life, an American school.

When we left our front door, his hand clung tightly to mine. As we drew closer to the school, his grip loosened by degrees. Finally, he saw a kid he recognized. "Hey, there's John. Hey, John!" He dropped my hand like a hot horseshoe and made his own way to his classroom, leaving me alone on the school grounds to watch my little boy go to school without me.

I don't look forward to these departures, these separations from parents. I don't anticipate with any enthusiasm at all my daughters' weddings, my son's mission farewell, my kids going away to school. I like having them around, hearing them breathing at night, rustling in their beds. I like seeing them wake up in the morning, saying morning prayers with them in the living room, hearing them play in the backyard on the trampoline with the sprinkler spraying them from beneath. I like the sweaty kid smell that emanates from the backs of their necks at the end of a hot summer day. I like seeing them with wet hair plastered to their heads when they come out of the shower or bath, smelling of soap and shampoo. I love talking to them at bedtime, getting a good-night kiss and a hug—or at least trying to get them from the teenaged kids.

It's inevitable, I know. Kids grow up. They leave home gradually, in short little bursts at first: a few nights at Grandma's house, then slumber parties, then girls' camp or Scout camp, then a school trip or two. The gulf widens: college, missions, marriage, careers. College and missions and marriage and jobs don't just take them out of the home, away from me, they take them out of state, maybe out of the country, definitely out of my life. They'll have their own Thanksgiving dinners, decorate their own Christmas trees, celebrate their birthdays—the days I'll remember them the most, without me, their father.

I often joke with my younger daughters that I don't want them to marry. I want them to stay home forever to take care of me when I'm old. I tell them that I'll chase away the boys who will come to see them, who will someday want to take them away from me.

I'm only half joking.

In a perfect world, my children would grow up and stay home, or if not at home, in a home just down the street or around the corner. In a perfect world, I would be the kind of father (and grandfather) who would not intrude on their lives, would not give advice where it's not wanted, would not expect them to be at my table for Thanksgiving and at my hearth for Christmas morning. I would let them raise their children, let them make the same mistakes I have made, let them be free when they want and need to be free, let them come home when they need and want to come home. I would not begrudge the men and women and institutions that take them from me. I would love those they love.

In a perfect world, my departed children would drop by my house on their way home from work or sometime after dinner just to chat or seek my advice. They would take my advice and prosper and be happy. They would visit me when I'm sick and stay by me to read, to soothe, or, just by their mere presence, to show support and love. They would name my grandchildren after me (not after *his* or *her* parents) and bring the little darlings to my house to let me spoil them rotten. They would not bring their children to me when I'm tired or cranky or not in the mood for children. They would remember my birthday and anniversary. They would visit me on *their* birthdays to thank me for being their father. They would turn down jobs, proposals, and schools that would take them away from me for too long or that would make them unhappy. All four of them would come over together sometimes—without spouses and children—and we would be the same old family again. We would look at old photos and family videos, pull out remembrance boxes and savor old memories, old events, the same old love.

Writing this, thinking this, makes me teary eyed. I love my children and know they love me. But I also know this isn't a perfect world. I dread the inevitable mission farewells and weddings and other ceremonies of separation because I know they will tear my heart out. After they've left home, I know that some of my children, maybe all of them, will not live down the street or around the corner. I know if they did, there would be times when they would think, "Oh, why did we ever move so close to *Dad?*" And there would be times when I might think the same thing. As adults, they will not have the relationship with me that they now have. They will be different people; I will be different too. They will forget many of the childhood moments: the late vacation nights in hotel rooms eating pizza and watching cable movies, after-dinner strolls and frolics along Temple Beach, the 2:00 A.M. bottles in the big wooden rocker, running upstairs from the "pinch monster" as he chased them to bed, lying on the trampoline at night watching for meteors, Saturday afternoon bike rides and picnics at Himeji Castle, getting a ride to school in a snowstorm, eating a hamburger and fries alone with Dad at the Cougareat, going to the grocery store to get necessities and treats—always some treats, snuggling up together on the big sofa eating popcorn and watching a video.

Certainly, some of these will, for one reason or another, remain etched in my children's memories. But as they grow older and live lives of their own, lives away from and separate from mine, their minds will fill with their own memories, the lives they create and live without me. These memories will crowd out many that we now share. On some special occasions when we're all gathered together, an anecdote will surface and that will resurrect a Dad-memory in one child, which will then trigger a recollection in another. The conversation will grow enthusiastic and nostalgic at the same time. Together they'll recall and enjoy moments they'd forgotten but which I will never, can never, forget.

Fortunately for me, those days are still some distance off. Right now, I've got them all around me. We're still making those memories, having the little experiences that one day they'll forget and I'll savor. And I'm savoring them right now, this very moment picturing my Carrie and Joanne, who will soon come running up the stairs and down the hall to my office. Before I actually see them, I'll hear the tromp-tromp of their footsteps and their giggling and panting as they race to my door. They'll tell me that Mom and everybody are out in the parking lot, waiting for me to join them for our picnic dinner at Rock Canyon.

They'll be here any minute. We'll go and have a good time, but in the back of my mind I'll still wish Christy would have called today; I'll still wish there was something I could do to delay the separation and departure, to keep them around me, to hold on to my children's childhood—to keep permanently my children my children.

I Wanted to Be
a Mirthwriter

My obsession with Mirthright began in Sister Morrell's creative writing class at BYU. "Really, Chris," she wrote on one of my papers, "you ought to send some of your work to the *Ensign*'s Mirthright. I'm sure they'd enjoy your sense of humor as much as I do."

So I sent the *Ensign* a funny anecdote. They sent it back. I sent some more. They rejected those too. I kept it up until it turned into a regular serve-and-volley exchange: I'd serve up a nice witty manuscript, and they'd fire it back so fast it made me dizzy.

A few years and many rejections later, the *Ensign* changed its Mirthright format from short anecdotes to humorous essays. Humorous essays being my forte, I welcomed the change. Finally, I'd be able to serve an ace.

My first Mirthright article was "Get Me Out of Scouting!" Fresh out of BYU, I, who had never been a Scout, was appointed assistant Scoutmaster, and the Scouts in my ward took full advantage of my ignorance. On our first camp out, they tricked me into chanting what they had convinced me was a very sacred ancient Indian chant, "O-wa ta-jur ki-am" ("Oh-what-a-jerk-I-am"). Things went downhill from there.

So, apparently, did my article. The Mirthrighters rejected it. My next attempt was "Murphy Must Have Been a Mormon."

It listed witty aphorisms for Mormon parents, like, "Kids will have tantrums only at Church, and the size of the audience has a direct effect on the violence and the duration of the tantrums," and "Grandparents will undo any disciplinary training you've given your children, and, when they're finished, they'll tell you what's wrong with your kids."

My article left out one Murphyism: An essay on Murphy's Law is bound to be rejected.

Over the years, I wrote and sent a bunch more; all came back with the same cold message of rejection: "Dear Writer, Thank you for sharing your work with us. Unfortunately, it does not fit into our current plans at this time."

It finally occurred to me that my experiences didn't have the right combination of humor and spiritual uplift to worm wholesome grins out of the somber Mirthright editors. The only way to create a manuscript that would fit into their current plans would be to wait for the perfect Mirthright experience.

With the patience of an Eskimo ice fisherman, I waited for the right moment, for the funny church experience that would get me a byline in the *Ensign*. It finally struck one Sunday shortly after we had moved to Japan.

"Daddy, potty!" Carrie announced to everyone within shouting distance of us in sacrament meeting. "Daddy! Potty!" she repeated more loudly, guaranteeing we'd make our exit with an audience.

Normally I didn't begrudge two-year-old Carrie her sacrament meeting potty trips, but on that particular Sunday I was scheduled to be the last speaker on the program. Liz was out of the chapel feeding Joanne, so I took Carrie and hoped I'd make it back in time for my talk.

In the bathroom, I nudged her toward the toilet stall and turned to comb my hair. I had just pulled out my comb when I heard a "click" behind me.

It wasn't your average door-closing click; it was an ominous, uh-oh, toilet-stall-locking kind of click that reminds you to never let a two-year-old do anything alone, especially in a bathroom minutes before you're supposed to speak in sacrament meeting.

As soon as it clicked, I knew there was going to be trouble, but I tingled all over as the inspiration whacked me like a quadruple combination. *This is it! This is my Mirthright experience.* I couldn't help grinning as I turned around to deal with the locked toilet stall door and the prisoner behind it.

"Carrie," I called through the door, "it's time to come out, honey." In reply she shoved her panties under the door.

"Carrie, this is Daddy. We've got to go back to church. Open the door, okay?" A hard knot of anxiety formed in my stomach. *My daughter's trapped in this toilet stall, I have a talk to give in a few minutes, and my Japanese translator's sitting alone on the stand with a copy of my talk in hand probably wondering if I had already been translated or had just chickened out at the last minute.*

"Carrie, unlock the door, please. I want to go to church." I heard her tugging on the lock. Of course, I knew it wouldn't open. If it had, this would have been just another not-quite-a-Mirthright experience.

The lock held. "Perfect," I chuckled to myself. "The *Ensign*'ll love this."

"Daddy. . . Daddy! Want out," Carrie cried, realizing her predicament.

I couldn't reach over the door, and she couldn't crawl under it. Carrie would have to open it herself, or I'd have to figure out some way to open it for her.

"Hang on, Carrie, I'll be right back," I called to her as I left the bathroom in search of a ladder or footstool.

I grabbed a chair from the Relief Society room and carried it back into the bathroom. Carrie grinned when she saw me looking down at her from atop the chair. "Hi, Daddy. Stuck." She pointed to the door.

"I know, babe. Unlock the door, 'kay? Push on that knob. That's it. No, the other way. 'Atta girl. No, push harder." She couldn't budge it, and even from my perch atop the chair, I couldn't reach it.

It's funny how your mind works at times like these. I should have been worrying about getting my daughter safely out of the toilet stall, about giving my sacrament meeting talk, about avoiding the huge potential for embarrassment that would permanently taint my family in this face-saving country if sacrament meeting were interrupted by the arrival of a phalanx of firefighters to rescue my female child from a toilet stall in the men's restroom of the only LDS church in a city of half a million. But I couldn't help smiling as I savored the experience. The article was already forming in my mind; several possible titles presented themselves: "Trapped in the Toilet" or "Not without *My* Daughter" or "Stalled in the Bathroom on the Way to a Sacrament Talk." It couldn't miss.

With the sounds of the beginnings of a Carrie tantrum echoing behind me, I hustled back to the Relief Society room and went through the closets looking for a broom or a pointer or anything long enough to reach the door's latch. Nothing. Next I tried the kitchen. The longest thing I could find was a large lacquer serving tray. It'd have to do.

When Carrie saw me back at my perch, she interrupted her tantrum long enough to kick the locked door a few times and to add a few more layers of toilet paper to the mound she had shredded while I was gone.

"It's okay, Carrie. I'll get you out." I lowered the serving tray—it wasn't quite long enough to reach the latch, so I stood tiptoe on the chair, one leg out for balance, and leaned over the top, teetering on my stomach as I hung headfirst down into the stall.

After a few swings of the tray, I connected, and the door popped open.

I hopped off the chair and handed Carrie her panties. "Put these back on, and I'll be right back." Hoping I still had time for my talk, I grabbed the chair and serving tray to return them.

On my way out the bathroom door, I ran into Sister Daimon and her three-year-old son in the hallway. "*Konnichi wa*" ("Good afternoon"), I said as I smiled and shuffled past her with the chair in one hand and the serving tray in the other. I didn't have the time or the Japanese to explain what I was doing with a Relief Society chair and serving tray in the bathroom.

Slightly rumpled and trailing shreds of toilet paper as we went, Carrie and I made it back to the chapel just in time to have the bishop introduce me as the last speaker.

The next night I sat at my word processor and wrote up "Trapped in the Toilet." It was one of those transcendent writing moments: everything fell into place so perfectly and quickly that my fingers could barely keep up with the inspiration that poured out of my mind like a tidal wave. I knew then what Handel must have felt like when he composed the *Messiah*.

As perfect as it was, I worked on my essay more the next week, rewriting and revising, fine tuning until it glowed, even shimmered. With just the right balance of humor and uplift, it was the perfect account of the perfect Mirthright experience. A wave of confidence washed over me as I dropped the completed and positively unrejectable manuscript into the mail; it would be only a matter of time before I'd hear the good news from the *Ensign*.

I was only half right. It was only a matter of time, but the news wasn't good. Four months after I had mailed my inspired tale, the *Ensign* returned it with their standard rejection slip. Obviously, my perfect Mirthright experience wasn't as perfect as I had thought.

Since then, the *Ensign* no longer publishes Mirthright essays. I take some comfort in that. I'm convinced that my toilet masterpiece must have created a huge split among the editorial staff, a veritable war in heaven, with the two-thirds wanting to publish "Trapped in the Toilet" and the one-third wanting to reject it. Rather than mediate a dispute that surely would have sent one-third of the host of *Ensign* editors looking for another job, the guy in charge obviously decided to restore the peace by announcing that they'd quit publishing Mirthright essays.

So my perfect manuscript lies dormant in my desk drawer, waiting for that great and glorious day when it can be resurrected. That day will come only when there's a major change in the *Ensign* editorial staff—perhaps when the humorless one-third has left to oppose fine writing at some other publication and Sister Morrell is appointed to take their place.

Feeling Small

I have an inferiority complex. It's not crippling, but it is a fairly steady pain, like a burr in my sock all day long.

Part of it I attribute to my birth order. I'm the third child of five, with two older brothers who have led charmed and charming lives. Confident and comfortable as cats, they walked a gilded path through our childhood: good at sports, at school, with friends. They went to good colleges, got good grades, and started good careers and families. Now one is president of a large junior college; the other is a successful football coach. I have always admired—okay, envied—them and their talents and successes. In many ways, I want to be like them, but it is clear to me now, as it was when I was a child, that if we were breakfast cereals, they'd be Wheaties and Sugar Frosted Flakes, and I'd be generic oatmeal.

Several other things contribute to my insecurities. My pedigrees, for example. At a college meeting last week, department leaders introduced their new faculty members, most of them cream-faced babes fresh from graduate schools. But not just any graduate schools—the best of the best. The names of the schools were a review of the Hall of Fame of Prestigious and Elite American Universities: USC, Harvard, Yale, Stanford, Cornell. In comparison, my academic pedigree is pretty pedestrian. I did my graduate work at Arizona State, a respectable but not renowned university.

I realize it's not my new colleagues' fault that they were brilliant enough and fortunate enough to graduate from some of the best institutions of higher learning in the galaxy. No, the fact that I'm a lesser light is clearly because I am dimmer than many of the bright young faculty currently being hired at BYU.

My family pedigree is equally as pedestrian, but it stings much more because I am reminded of it with distressing regularity. I was blissfully ignorant of my deficiency until I had been a member of the Church for a few years. After a time, I discovered I was excluded, unintentionally, from the common types of introductory dialogue Lifetime Mormons participate in when they meet a stranger.

From what I have observed, it goes like this:

Setting: Somewhere in Utah, the recent latter days.

Two Lifetime Mormon men meet for the first time. They each tuck their day planners under their left arms and shake hands briskly. After a brief exchange of greetings, their conversation begins.

Lifetime Mormon 1: So, where are you from?

Lifetime Mormon 2: Springville.

LTM 1: Really? Well, then, you must know FamousPioneerName.

LTM 2: Oh yes, he's my uncle. Actually, he's my wife's uncle. My mother was a PioneerName, and her people didn't come down to Springville until 1880. How about you?

LTM 1: Well, I'm from FamousPioneerSettlement. My great-great-grandfather, ReallyFamousPioneerName, settled there in 1865. He was a polygamist, so I've got tons of ReallyFamousPioneerName cousins.

LTM 2: Then do you know AnotherFamousPioneerName?

LTM 1: He's my uncle!

LTM 2: You don't say? He was my mission president when I served in England.

LTM 1: I served my mission in Scotland. So did my father and grandfather. All our people are from there. My great-great-grandfather came over the plains in one of the first handcart companies.

LTM 2: I thought he settled in YetAnotherFamousPioneer-Settlement.

LTM 1: He did, but Brigham Young asked my great-grandfather to go down to FamousPioneerSettlement, where he met and married YetAnotherReallyFamousPioneerName and started raising a family.

The conversation goes on from there, the two Lifetime Mormons comparing roots and genealogies, hometowns and histories, dropping whole bushel baskets full of pioneer family and place-names.

But here's how it goes when a Lifetime Mormon meets *me* for the first time:

LTM: So, where are you from?
Me: Well, I've lived kinda all over, but I was born in Danville, Illinois.
LTM: [puzzled momentarily, then says brightly] Really? That anywhere near Carthage?
Me: Nope.
LTM: [growing uncomfortable] Nauvoo?
Me: Actually, it's pretty near Chicago.
LTM: [now bored with the conversation] Chicago, huh? Well, it was nice meeting you . . . uh, what did you say your name was again?

It's become clear to me that as a convert from outside of Utah, it's impossible to participate in these kinds of cultural-genealogical conversations. My genealogy has only been traced back four generations on my dad's side. On my mom's Norwegian side, we're stuck at three. None of them were Mormon pioneers. None trekked across the plains. None ever set foot in Utah. To handicap me even further, I know barely enough Church history to fill up a Sunday School lesson; I know even less about Utah and its many obscure little pioneer towns. I can't tell Vernon from Vernal, Centerville from Orderville, Heber City from Brigham City. (My kids will probably never amount to anything in Utah, and it will be my fault because I'm not a Son of Utah Pioneer and because I can't find Mt. Pleasant on a map.) I know Lifetime Mormons don't intend to be unkind or exclusionary, but being unable to take part in this important introductory ritual makes me feel like I'm out of the loop, a lost generation, a Gentile in Zion, an orphan at a family reunion.

A friend of mine—the same friend who, during general conference priesthood sessions, leans over as nearly every speaker concludes and whispers with a nod, "He's my relative"—calls me "genealogically challenged." And I suppose he's right. I often do wish that I were connected to some large clan, that I were a leaf on the branch of a proud and prolific pioneer family tree. It would be nice to swap small pioneer town names with strangers. I would enjoy playing genealogical one-upmanship with people I meet and casually dropping my trump card at the end of our dialogue: a family connection with an Apostle or prophet.

But I can't. I'm handcart handicapped, descendant disabled, genealogically challenged. And when my thin and obscure family shrub brushes up against one of the great and mighty redwoods of the pioneer lore, well, I can't help but feel dwarfed, envious, inferior.

My Lifetime Mormon friends who know of my affliction try in vain to comfort me. "Hey, you're a convert, a pioneer yourself." Yeah, right. You'll notice, as I always do, that they say "pioneer" with a little *p*.

But my inferiority complex is fostered by more than just my puny pedigrees. I am awed by the truly incredible people I know. At the end of a long day, when I've collapsed into my La-Z-boy to watch *Roseanne* reruns before going to bed, I think of these people. They certainly are not camped out in front of the TV rotting their brains and senses with sitcoms. No, they're out jogging. Or reading the Book of Mormon with their kids. Or writing in their journals. Or helping their sons with Eagle Scout projects. Or doing genealogy. Or sitting in Church meetings. Or taking inventory of their food storage.

There's Brother W. down the road. He's forty-five but looks thirty. He runs marathons, serves as bishop of his ward, and maintains an acre of impeccable lawn and garden. His kids are smart and wonderful and successful. And there's Professor W. (no relation to Brother W.) in my department. He's spiritual, kind, sensitive, and thoroughly charitable. He's also brilliant, productive, and charismatic. Year after year he receives awards and superior ratings for his teaching.

And there's Professor E., who writes books in the same time it takes me to write paragraphs. He's profoundly wise, has read everything, and understands everything. And he's purely Christian, completely and seriously a Latter-day Saint. There's Professor P., also in my department. She is electrifyingly vivacious. Students flock to her classes and revel in her talent and wit. Her books are polished and popular and funny. She's polished, popular, and funny. And there are others around me, so many others, that are so brilliant, so talented, so Christian, so purely wonderful that I feel like the pauper at the palace when I'm around them. I love these people, love associating with them, love learning from them. These people are top sirloin; I am high-fat ground beef.

I know it's wrong to have these kinds of puny feelings, these stunted ego musings. I don't have them all the time. And despite how I might sound, I don't begrudge the Midases and Mozarts and Einsteins around me their talents and accomplishments. Truth be told, I really don't envy them either (that's because I know that it's *wrong* and unhealthy to envy others—and I don't need to add guilt to my inferiority complex). But I do see in these people what I aspire to be but am not, and it hurts.

So I keep working at it, as most fathers do. Losing a pound here, a bad habit there. Working a little harder, learning a little more. The scripture in the Doctrine and Covenants (I just had to go look it up—if I were more like these people, I would have known it already), "line upon line, precept upon precept; here a little, and there a little; giving us consolation by holding forth that which is to come, confirming our hope!" gives me some hope, some encouragement. It's a salve for my inferiority complex. Things take time. Pioneer trees don't sprout overnight. It takes eons of pressure for a chunk of coal to turn into a diamond. I suppose—no, I know—that that's part of the reason we're taught about eternal progression. I just hope it won't take me that long to catch up with these people.

It'll be nice, someday, to join their ranks.

The Countdown

I just called Time and Temperature to verify it: in one hour, eight minutes, and forty seconds my life will change. Like a snake sloughing off its scaly old skin, I'm sloughing off some old, but instead of coming out of it shiny and new, I'm going to be older, wrinklier, grayer, paunchier. Minus a few brain cells, plus a few pounds.

My body has been gearing up for this for some time. Just a couple days ago, for example, I was looking over my wife's shoulder as she read the mail. Standing there, nothing in my hands, no strenuous activity, no sudden movement, no bad angles. Wham—the bony finger of the Grim Reaper reached out and touched my back just below the right shoulder blade. Crick. Ache. Knot. It still hurts. Liz says I should see a chiropractor. Buy a weight set. Don't let the kids walk on it.

I take Tylenol.

It still hurts.

Jonathan walks on it. Carrie kneels on it. I stretch and do push-ups and sit-ups and go jogging.

It still hurts.

I'm not crippled by it. It's just a dull, annoying ache, one that feels like all I need to do to get rid of it is stretch and push in just the right way—a quick shrug of the shoulders, maybe, with a sideways tilt of the head would pop that old disk or vertebra or whatever it is right back into place.

But I know it won't.

It's a wake-up call: my body is telling me to gear up for the long, slow decline, the one that eventually ends in a casket. I'm going to be a step slower, stay sick longer, get tired faster, see my temper get shorter.

Fifty-eight minutes, forty seconds left.

Even my typing's slower.

A few months ago I hit a physical peak. I'd get up at 5:05 A.M. and run two and a half, maybe three miles. Then I'd join Liz for a half hour of aerobics. Three afternoons a week, I played racquetball. Weight melted off my midsection like butter on a hot ear of corn. My pants loosened up. I cinched in my belt to notches not seen in years. I needed less sleep, less food. I was cruising away from Old Man Time and the baggage of burdens he throws on us as we age.

Then I got sick.

The weight returned faster than a bad check. My belt slipped back to its former comfortable notch. I was sleepy and hungry all the time.

Wake-up call: "You're not getting any younger, bud. As a matter of fact, things don't move in *that* direction, old fella. They move only one way—down."

It's crept up on me in other ways too. A month ago an old high school pal called and told me his oldest son is in college. Another high school friend is a *grand*father. Nolan Ryan's retired. There simply are no professional athletes my age anymore. Guys my age are holding down responsible positions in government. They're stake and mission presidents, CEOs. They're building humongous houses and sending their kids to college and on missions. They're doing what they set out to do, what they've worked to do, what they were born to do.

Up to this point in my life, I have almost always been the kid: the youngest guy on the team. The youngest faculty member. The youngest high priest. No more. Now I'm one of the established guys. Some of the new people at work are young enough to have been my high school students. I'm old enough to be the father to some of my students. Young couples moving into the ward aren't just young, they're babies. Initially I feel connected to them, mistakenly thinking, *Hey, I'm like you—young, new to all this.* But then I look at them closely:

no wrinkles, no gray hairs, no kids, no mortgage. Just young pups at the pound.

These days I think of things I never thought I would think of and no longer think of things that used to occupy my mind constantly. There was a time, longer ago than I like to remember, that all I thought of was romance. Okay, that's not *all* I thought of, but it occupied a good chunk of my time. Those were the premarriage, honeymoon, and post-honeymoon days. Romance, love, passion. I left notes around the house. Bought flowers. Cooed romantic and seductive phrases into Elizabeth's ear. And planned rendezvous. Premeditated them. Anticipated them.

But that's gone now. Not the love, and certainly not the pleasure of romance—both of those have quadrupled over the years—but the mental preoccupation. It's just a mere shadow of its former self.

In its place have tromped in worries about work and money and kids. I calculate retirement benefits and savings accounts in my head. I wonder—no, I worry—that each new pain is only the beginning of something sinister and bad and terminal. Just last weekend, in preparation for tomorrow, I went on a long run, long for me, at least: almost eight miles up Hobble Creek Canyon and back. About halfway up I felt a tight little twinge in my upper left chest. A sharp but small pain. *Oh, no. I'm up here in the canyon without a single bit of ID,* I thought. *If a stroke or heart attack drops me, whoever finds me will have no idea who I am.*

Isn't that crazy?

Twenty years ago I wouldn't have even noticed the pain, let alone connected it to possible myocardial infarction. These days a new ache in the elbow signals the onset of rheumatoid arthritis. Throbbing knees warn of future knee replacements. Blurred vision isn't just a dirty contact lens, it's early glaucoma. New moles are pre-melanoma. Stomachaches are ulcers.

And what adds to the misery is the reminder that I'm not merely neurotic or hypochondric or paranoid but that I'm aging. Times are coming, have come, when there are some things I simply no longer can do. Some opportunities have passed and will never return. Some activities will for the rest of my life be only pleasant memories. And even then, if I'm unlucky, as time goes on and the brain cells don't, even those pleasant memories will be mere pleasant memories, if I manage to have any memory at all.

Twenty-eight minutes, forty seconds left.

I don't mean to be preoccupied with this. There was a time a few months ago when I looked forward to this day, to aging gracefully. I figured, in that upbeat time, *Hey, the last twenty years have been darn good, and then I was only learning. Now I've got the wisdom, experience, and time to really make use of the next twenty years. This is going to be great!*

But right now my eyes feel dry and achy. My back feels like there's a bruise under the shoulder blade. My feet are cold. My nose itches. I can feel the subtle but steady pull of gravity on the roll of flesh that's hanging over the elastic waistband of my sweatpants. I'm not seeing things through Pollyanna's eyes right now. As a matter of fact, I'm a tad blurry just now. Contacts in too long. Or glaucoma?

My body's telling me that I'm up an hour past my bedtime. I'll pay for this in the morning, I know. That apple fritter I ate after dinner will tangle with my lower intestines at about three in the morning. I'll wake up feeling drowsy and hung over, regretting my overindulgence at dinner and my piggishness at dessert. I'll tell myself that I know I'll feel better if I take a little jog but I won't have the gumption to get out of bed to do it. I'll sleepwalk through the morning and by three o'clock in the afternoon will kick myself for wasting away the day.

Somebody's up in the kitchen now. I hear the fridge door open and close. I bet it's Christy. She slept in this morning and probably can't sleep. I should go see what she's doing, if she needs anything, but I want to stay at my keyboard and document this evolutionary moment, to write my way right smack into it and see, at the actual turning point, what happens. Will I feel any different? Will I look any different? Will I be less neurotic, obsessed, morbid about the whole thing?

Eighteen minutes left.

I'm slowing down. Getting tired. This is rambling, the thoughts of a madman late at night with a large apple fritter lodged in his gut cutting off blood to his brain.

I don't want to become too morose. It's not the end of the world. People have been here and gone on. Lots of them have done great things, happy things even, after passing this milestone.

So can I. This isn't the last essay I will write, and with any luck, this will, after I take several revision shots at it, be much better than it is at this moment, filled with typos, non sequiturs, and fragmented thoughts.

I feel a little dizzy. Too many potato chips at dinner. Those plus the soda pop plus the apple fritter—it's all too much for my sluggish bloodstream to handle. At this very moment, large chunks of fat cells are being deposited in places where they're least needed and most noticed. At my age, you'd think I'd have developed a little self-control, that I'd have the discipline, and at least the good sense, to say no to things that make me feel (and look) fat, that make me feel fuzzy-headed and sluggish tonight and the next morning, that put my liver into overtime cranking out enough bile to digest all that's been thrown its way.

Where was I? Oh yeah. I was going to be positive.

Okay. At this point, I've got a decent salary. Liz just started a great part-time job, so things aren't so tight. We can go out to eat once in a while without feeling the pinch (except in my waistline). I can buy a new shirt or pair of shoes (which reminds me, I need to get a new pair of running shoes. Something with a good cushion so I don't wear out my knees before their time). Our savings are growing. We've got a couple of solid investments. The kids are healthy. I just had a novel published, and, with any luck, this will end up in print somewhere too. Liz and I have been married almost twenty-one years—twenty-one glorious, happy years. My mortgage is at 7.5 percent. The van's only got fourteen thousand miles on it. Jonathan had straight As this last grading period. My classes are going okay. The students are learning and seem fairly enthusiastic.

Seven and a half minutes left.

I genuinely like my job and the people I work with. Joanne was just baptized two weeks ago. Carrie just performed in *Swan Lake*. I ordained Jonathan a deacon six months ago.

Christy just made the varsity marching band. I've managed a fairly regular jogging routine for many months. My parents were just here for a visit, their first to Utah, and they liked it. I've visited two out of three of my home teaching families and still have three days left to visit the last one. My Sunday School class is going well. I like the kids, and they seem to be learning something.

Two minutes left.

Time is fast approaching. What will it be like? New Year's? No, no fireworks. No kiss and wishes for the next; Liz is already in bed, asleep.

Less than a minute. What will my last thoughts be?

I feel fat, overweight, tired. But I am glad to be working on this, to at least be doing something productive.

Two seconds.

That's it. I'm forty. I've just entered the forties. This all started in Danville, Illinois, on May 28, 1954. Now I'm sitting here in Springville, Utah, writing this and thinking these thoughts.

The only sounds I hear are the clicks of the keyboard and the annoying drone of the computer fan. A wind has just kicked up outside. It rained a while ago, and I can hear the whoosh and splatter as cars drive past our house. There's a slight ringing in my ears—has it always been there? I sigh. I'm going to the bathroom to take a look at my old self and see what's there.

Be right back.

Here's me at forty. (Forty? Man, how long will *that* take to get used to?)

The first thing I noticed is hair. Nose hairs primarily. Where did they all come from, and why can't they stay in my nostrils where they belong? Am I going to be a doddering old man with obnoxiously long and unkempt nose hairs? Is that what my grandkids are going to remember about me? And I have little white hairs, five or six of them, growing out of the base of each ear canal. Wiry things. Good grief. My sideburns have little glints of *silver* in them. Not enough to fret about, but their presence is notable. The skin above my eyelids sags a little, making it look like I've got double eyelids. I've got a day's growth of beard. Spotty. To the sides of my eyes I've got lines, wrinkles I suppose, shooting out in rays towards my ears. A red spot on my lower left cheek is a reminder that even middle-aged men can get zits. My forehead carries a few scars: chicken pox from days I can't recall. A pair of neat round little ones from a swan dive from an upper bunk when I was six. Another divot just off center on my left cheek came at age three from the metal nut on a toy phone. A kind of gouge to the left of center on my forehead is from my Cougar days when my football helmet didn't fit properly. That mole on my neck is sprouting a patch of black hairs like weedy Bermuda grass. A good sign, I guess.

The world is still turning. People are suffering terribly in Rwanda, Bosnia-Herzegovina, and even here in the land of plenty. Bill Clinton is the president. Ezra Taft Benson—I remember the day we stood and sustained him as prophet, seer, and revelator—is still the President of the Church. Rex Lee is running BYU; LaVell Edwards is running BYU's most prominent program. Jackie Kennedy just died. Flags remain at half-mast to mark Richard Nixon's passing. My aunt has bone cancer.

And I'm forty. Still here. Still at this keyboard. Still in this big old house surrounded by Liz and Christy, Jonathan, Carrie, and Joanne. The last four decades have been eventful ones, exciting ones, unpredictable ones. I wouldn't trade any part of them for anything. I'm looking forward to the next twoscore years with the hope—now I'm feeling upbeat again—that they'll be even better than the first forty. I'm going to give them my best shot. That's about all I can do. I'm just thankful—truly and honestly and completely thankful—to have this time, to have these opportunities, to have these blessings. It could be better, could have been better, I suppose, but I can't very well imagine how.

I'm tired. I'm forty. I'm going to bed.

The Little Plumbers

Every father ought to read the book of Job once in a while. Why? Because we often need the patience of Job. There are days—you know what I'm talking about—when if it's not one thing, it's another. You wake up late, cut yourself shaving, miss breakfast, and get to work late, a speck of toilet paper still on your bloody chin. You find out about the important meeting you were supposed to attend an hour *after* the meeting's over. Your desk looks like someone detonated a paper bomb on it, and you spend most of your day trying, in vain, to find the Very Important Papers you're sure you left there yesterday. The freeway on the way home moves like the Cougar Stadium parking lot at homecoming. You get home late for the fifth time that week, after you *promised* your wife, guaranteed, that you'd be home on time tonight for sure. And now that you're home, all you want to do is eat dinner, slink into the living room, and hide behind the newspaper for a while, then go to bed.

But—and you know what I'm talking about if you have kids—you can't, or don't dare, do that. They need someone to tell them to turn the TV down, help with homework, provide a ride to Mutual, cough up money for tomorrow's field trip, referee squabbles, and, when they're little, provide constant supervision. Older kids have their own ways of getting into trouble, but it's usually outside of the home; little ones can make mountains of headaches right in the privacy of their own home. Those are the days when you need Job's patience.

I've had my share of such days, but one from several years ago remains etched in my mind like a kid's handprint on a newly poured patio. In those days, Christy and Jonathan liked to team up for fun and mischief while I read the paper and Liz was busy with dinner. Christy was four, Jonathan was two, so she called the shots.

That evening's shots were called from the bathroom, where the two little plumbers had locked themselves to splash, play, and generally enjoy a little kid's life without any annoying interruptions from Liz or me.

An ominous silence (*all* silences in a house with two kids under five are ominous)—followed by a series of toilet flushes, giggles, and gurgles—alerted Liz and me to the scene. When we crashed their indoor beach party, the kids, the floor, and the walls were drenched with toilet water. Jonathan's yellow bathtub boat bobbed in the gentle tide of the toilet bowl, while the two little culprits, dripping with wide-eyed innocence, tried to explain what had happened.

Liz and I had been in the parenting game long enough not to be fooled by a couple of cherubic looks; the overwhelming circumstantial evidence condemned them on the spot. We disinfected them, spanked them, and sent them outside to safer and drier activities. The evening wore on, as evenings do; the bathroom returned to normal; and we forgot about the incident.

Later that night when I revisited the damp disaster area, it was obvious that somebody (or somebodies) hadn't been flushing the toilet. I didn't think much of it—after all, an unflushed toilet isn't all that unusual in a house inhabited by a four-year-old—and gave the toilet handle a yank.

The tank gurgled, the bowl bubbled, but instead of whirling everything neatly down the toilet drain, the murky water rose over the lip of the bowl, splashed onto the floor and over my bare feet.

I hopped from one foot to the other, yelling for Liz. When she came to the bathroom door, she looked at me sitting on the bathroom counter, my feet dripping wet; at the mess on the floor; and at the steady stream of water spilling over the edge of the toilet bowl.

"Toilet's clogged," she said.

As she stood in the safety of the hallway, I sat on the sink, and together we watched until the water ceased its relentless sludge over the edge of the toilet bowl.

To make a long, grimy story short, the plumber's friend, coat hanger, and Playtex-gloved hand (guess whose hand?) couldn't unplug our toilet again. I knew that on the morrow I would have two unpleasant alternatives: call a plumber and blow a chunk of our savings in one grand flush, or attack the problem myself with screwdriver, wrench, and my bare hands.

I decided to tackle it myself. If it was simple I'd be able to do the job and save the cost of a plumber. If it was complicated, I was sure to make it worse, guaranteeing that the plumber would earn his pay.

That evening around bedtime, as I was contemplating the day's disaster, Christy walked through my room on her way to use *our* toilet. On her way back to her room, I asked her about the day's flooding, hoping to discover what I'd be up against in the next day's amateur plumber hour.

"Christy, 'member when you and Jonathan were playing in the bathroom today?"

She didn't answer. Even a four-year-old knows better than to incriminate herself.

"C'mon," I wheedled, "you're not in trouble now. Do you remember when you two were playing in the toilet?"

She nodded.

"Did you put anything in there besides the boat?"

"Nope," she answered cautiously. "We were just washing it."

"So you didn't put anything else in there? No toys? No dolls? No shoes?"

"No, Daddy. We were just washing the boat."

"Did you use washcloths?"

"Just two."

"Which two?"

"The ones from the hall closet."

"What happened to them?"

"But, Daddy, we were just using 'em to wash the boat . . . one is still okay. I put it back in the closet."

"Still wet?"

"Uh-huh, but I did put it away."

"Great." (Job's patience kicks in about here.) "What about the other?" I asked, anticipating the awful answer.

"It drownded."

Worrying About Babies

When you're a new husband, a naive and glassy-eyed newlywed, you worry about the dumbest things. Of course, I worried about the usual stuff—money, getting out of school, getting into a job, keeping my teeth flossed—but for some inexplicable reason I also used to worry that the IRS would audit us and we'd lose everything in tax court even though we didn't really *have* anything. In my new-husband nightmares, I imagined myself an innocent victim of the IRS bureaucracy and the heartless court system, yanked from the bosom of my new bride and planted in a dank prison cell for my first few anniversaries.

I also used to worry inordinately about proper bathroom etiquette. Not just the little things like where to keep my razor and shaving cream and how often I should wipe out the wad of hair from the shower drain, but about the big things. Would my bride consider it rude, gross, grounds for divorce, if I read *Sports Illustrated* in the bathroom? And even more important, would she seek an annulment if she entered the bathroom too soon after one of my reading sessions?

Perhaps less neurotic was my fear that we would have too many children too soon. As poor married students, our insurance was the bare bones, major medical-catastrophic kind: medical complications resulting from nuclear fallout, Brazilian rain forest contaminants, or the Andromeda Strain, or common ailments started on February 29 would be covered generously, *after* we paid a $1500 deductible. Regular stuff like office visits, hospitalization, surgical procedures, and especially obstetrics were covered only after a deductible the size of the national debt.

So the worst case scenario, as I saw it, was that Elizabeth would get pregnant in our first months of marriage. She'd be carrying twins or triplets, and they'd have to be delivered cesarean during finals week. She and the babies would be fine, but I'd flunk out of school and end up working graveyard shifts at 7-11 for the rest of my life to pay off the medical bills. And, of course, because we were young, healthy, and passionate, we'd keep on having kids at the rate of one or so per year for ten to fifteen years. We'd be perpetually penniless; I'd work day and night, my wife would be end up like the Old Woman Who Lived in a Shoe, and the kids would mill around our ramshackle rented house wearing tattered clothes, grimy faces, and hungry looks.

Ironically, overpopulation was a problem we never had to deal with. After two years of marriage we remained kidless and started to worry that maybe we'd never have any children. That's when my wife started talking about adoption.

"Are you kidding?" I'd say. "We'll have plenty when the time's right, and besides, I want my firstborn to be my own flesh and blood." Spoken like a true, but stupid, patriarch.

For some reason, the prospect of adoption worried me more than the threat of being overrun and run down by a relentless stream of Crowe babies. I know now that it was an irrational worry, but it was a palpable one, one infinitely more real and intimidating than IRS incarceration or bathroom *faux pas*. Part of my worry came from the macho flesh-and-blood lust in me. After all, everybody knows that a real man fathers real children, children who'll inherit his genes, his foibles, his moles and hair color. Adopting children would be denying this machismo, would amount to admitting wimpishness, giving up hope that my wife and I ever would pool genes to create our next generation.

I worried about the social and family consequences as well. No Crowe that I knew of had ever adopted a child. What would my parents and siblings think of me if I were the first?

And if they could get over my break with tradition, would they ever fully accept adopted children into the family? We were already relative pariahs because we were Mormons; would the added unconventionality of adopting children put us even farther on the fringe of the family circle? And what of my friends? Would they think I had become some sort of social crusader, someone who takes in strays and rejects in hopes of bolstering my own inadequacies? Would my football teammates think me less a man because I had to adopt children?

And of course, I worried about the potential adoptees. Many of the adopted kids I had known as a child were odd and dysfunctional (at least to me, but then, I was probably odd and dysfunctional too). Selfishly, I worried that we might be saddled with children who would spend their lives making me miserable, causing me embarrassment, shame, and expense. I also worried that my adopted children might not accept *me*. No matter how much I loved and cared for them, what if they never bonded to me, never accepted me as their father?

I also worried about the expense. The adoption fee was high, exorbitant for a young married couple, and in those days not a dime of it was tax deductible. How could we possibly absorb the cost, manage to pay all the household bills, and still have enough left over to raise a family?

A few years passed, and my neuroses and I kept the idea of adoption at a safe, abstract distance. But after a couple more years with no pregnancies but lots of tests, temperature charts, pills, and even a couple surgeries, it was looking more and more like a flesh-and-blood edition of Chris Crowe might never come off the assembly line. So when my wife again brought up the possibility of adoption, I was more open to the idea than I had ever been. Maybe it was maturity, maybe desperation, maybe just plain old common sense. I wanted to be a father, to leave behind a goodly posterity, and I realized that I wanted to have my firstborn child at least a few years sooner than Father Abraham had his.

It was a long, expensive process, one filled with interviews and paperwork and anticipation. Two years after we filed, our first child was born. We met Christy in a quiet office at LDS Social Services. She was delivered to us with ease. We endured no mood swings, no morning sickness, no maternity clothes, no Lamaze classes, no weight gain, no labor pains. We knew the first time we saw her, the first time we held her, the first time we heard her cry that she was our baby, our daughter, a miracle child delivered to us the way Heavenly Father wanted it. Two years later Jonathan arrived at the same small office at Social Services. Two years after that, Carrie was born, and just a year after her, Joanne became the final Crowe to join our nest.

No more worries. No doubts. These four are *my* kids. I don't know where the old concerns went, or why, but the moment I first saw Christy, all my adoption worries evaporated. I have never doubted that these children are my children, not my "adopted" children but *my* children, born and delivered to my wife and me, sealed to us. When we lived in Japan we met Barbara Smith, former Relief Society General President, at stake conference. From the stand, our family, one of the few *gaijin* families in the Japanese congregation, was pretty obvious, but so was the fact that our two youngest children have a mixed racial background. After the meeting we talked with her briefly; she mentioned that she assumed our children were adopted. "You know," she said, "I've been thinking an awful lot about adoption lately, and I think the Lord looks on it very positively." She went on to point out that Jesus was more or less adopted by Joseph and that members of the Church are adopted into the house of Israel. I appreciated her sensitivity and observations, but my wife and I had reached those same conclusions long ago. Unfortunately, some people can't see it that way. These people worry more about adoption and my children than I ever did.

When Christy was still a new baby, a ward member admired her briefly and then said to my wife, "You know, I'm amazed that you guys are willing to take in a strange baby. I know you must love her and all that, but since you're not her natural mother, you'll never really be able to have any maternal feelings or instincts."

Others have tried to be complimentary about our new kids, but their comments have only shown us how little they understand adoption. They're the ones who admired our cute little baby and said, "We really admire you for adopting. It must be an awful challenge."

I guess I'm glad some people admire us for adopting, but I'm always curious why they feel that they should admire us. Would they make a similar comment to other new parents? "Gee, my wife and I sure admire you for having a baby." It really doesn't take any more courage to adopt a child than it does to have one naturally. It does take a little more advance planning and paperwork, but when all's said and done, the results are the same.

And because our last two children have a racially mixed background, we received the usual adoption comments plus a few more. "Cute baby. Uh, what nationality is she?"

For some reason, this question annoys me more than all the rest. Maybe I'm just overly sensitive, maybe I think it's none of their business, maybe I'm just plain cranky, but I rarely give a straight answer to this question. I worry just as much about my children's ethnic background as my father worried about mine. Maybe I should be concerned about helping them appreciate their native ethnic heritage, maybe I should gladly blab to all the world that my children are this percent that and this percent this. But I'm their father, their flesh-and-blood father, and when I look at them all I see is my children. I'm color blind and I guess I wish everyone else were too. Of course I understand, as my children do, that they had birth parents who are not their current parents, and we all appreciate their birth parents' sacrifice. But my wife and I are their real parents just as they are our real children. We feel no need to call them our "adopted" children or our "ethnic-label" children any more than we would refer to my mother's mother as my "Norwegian" grandmother or to my dad as my "natural" father.

I'd like to say that most of the unthinking comments and questions about my children and adoption don't bother me— after all, I used to be a flesh-and-blood man myself—but I'd be lying. They *do* bother me. I appreciate people who see our family as a unit—the Crowes—not as Chris and Elizabeth and their four adopted children. My children are just that—*my* children. They're sealed to my wife and me, they live with us, they've been raised by us. Sure, they came into our family a little differently than other children get to their families, but in our case it was the only way we could have gotten together. Thanks to their birth parents and to LDS Social Services, the Lord found another way to send them to us.

I know I'm sermonizing here, but a child's parents aren't necessarily the ones who teamed up to conceive it; just about anybody can *make* a baby. Parents are the people who change diapers and stay up for 2:00 A.M. feedings and colic. They're the ones who train the children, worry about them, love them, care for them, sacrifice for them, and provide for them. *That's* parenthood, and that's what my wife and I are trying to provide for our foursome. So who cares if we're not their biological parents? Christy, Jonathan, Carrie, and Joanne are ours familially, legally, and eternally. And my only worry now is to make sure I do everything I can to keep it that way.

Chrissy the Sissy

Juliet, trying to reassure Romeo that she wouldn't let the feud between their families come between them, said: "What's in a name? That which we call a rose by any other word would smell as sweet."

She was wrong, dead wrong. Some names stink.

Names are terribly important things. A right name lubricates and cushions the twists and turns in life. A wrong name is a lifelong burr under your saddle. That's why, as a father, I was very careful about what Liz and I named our children. I didn't want my son to be so ashamed of his name that he'd go through his entire life calling himself the Brother of Christy. Likewise, I didn't want my daughters coming to me in ten years to say, "Dad, I hate my name," or to ask, "Would you care if I changed my name to something else?" Growing up is tough enough without having a nerdy name to add to life's woes.

I realize that times change, and so does language, but with the language being what it is today, I would never name a kid of mine Gay, nor would I label one of my own James (can you imagine being called Jim Crowe all your life?). There are other names which in and of themselves are perfectly fine—some of my best friends have them—that I would never use for my kids. My children will have plenty of trials of their own making, and I didn't want to make matters worse by giving them names that would be mispronounced, misspelled, or ridiculed for most of their lives.

Before you think I'm a little cracked about names, let me explain that I'm speaking from experience. My first name has been butchered, sliced, and diced in just about every way imaginable. I'm sure my parents meant well enough, but there have been many times when I've wished they would have thought twice about christening me Chris.

Actually, my first name is Christopher, as in St. Christopher, and that wasn't bad for starters. As a Catholic kid, I thought Christopher was a solid, reputable Catholic name. But when I was in fifth grade, the Catholic Church announced that St. Christopher had never really existed, and they stripped him of his sainthood. So despite all the stories I had been taught about my now decanonized namesake in Catholic school, I was stuck without a patron saint to call my own: my first identity crisis.

Still, I've always been interested in my name, and when I got older I did a little research on it, hoping to find out that it meant "wonderful child" or "man of strength" or something else I could brag about to my friends. The dictionary said that it is Greek for "Christ bearer." Not exactly something I could brag about on the playgrounds. Another book said that Christopher was ranked second among the top fifty boys' names, but that didn't make me feel any better either. It just meant thousands of other kids were suffering for their names' sake just as much as I was.

The suffering was rarely in the form of physical abuse. Most often it was a kind of rhyming, name-twisting game played by other kids at school to see exactly how many ways they could contort my name into something derogatory or inflammatory. The curse of Christopher is that its short form, Chris, can also be a girl's name, something my classmates were well aware of. "Chrissy the Sissy" was by far the most popular name transformation, and the sissy tag was reinforced by my alliterative initials, "C.C.," leaving me a doubly doomed sissy. My initials also contributed to mocking calls of "Sí, sí, Señor C.C." during recess. "Crisco Oil," a variation on Chris Crowe, ran a close second to "Chrissy the Sissy." In those days I longed for a plain, macho, incontortable name like Mike or John or Tom. I even talked to my parents about it, but legal name changing was too expensive, they said, and they assured me that the teasing would stop when my friends matured a little.

Things did get better in high school. By then most people knew me well enough to stop calling me "Chrissy the Sissy" (though one classmate inexplicably called me Bruce all through school). Being 6′3″ and over 200 pounds helped. Of course, it might have also been due to the fact that in my high school, no one except teachers ever called a kid by his first name. And that was fine with me. While in high school I happily answered to Crowe and almost forgot about my sissy first name.

But in the last three months of my senior year, a new form of name abuse began: I started receiving recruiting letters from prestigious women's colleges in the East and Midwest, all addressed to "Miss Chris Crowe." I still occasionally receive letters addressed to "Miss Chris Crowe" or "Ms. Chris Crowe" (Liz and I flip a coin over letters addressed to "Mrs. Chris Crowe"), but those don't bother me nearly as much as they did when I was waiting for my voice to change and my peach fuzz to turn into a beard.

Unfortunately, the misuse of my name hasn't been limited to the gender confusion of my youth. Orthographic variation, a fancy-schmancy name for creative spelling, has also turned my name inside out. I often wonder if anyone besides my wife, my mom, and me can spell "Chris" correctly. Judging from the variant spellings I've received in the mail over the years, I doubt it: Cris, Chis, Kris, Kriss, even Kurees.

Another permutation of my first name comes regularly from BYU. The official alumni magazine, requests for donations, and promotional literature I get from my alma mater, which ought to know better, address me as "Christophe Crowe." Magazines, junk mailers, and others who use a computer to print my one-letter-too-many first name treat me the same way. One computer labeler, bless its little CPU, came up with a creative solution. It kicked out a letter to "Mr. Christophe Rcrowe." I appreciated the effort.

When I got married, my first name tribulations didn't get any better, they merely spread to my wife. Her name's Elizabeth, I call her Liz, but for some reason many of our friends call her Chris. Maybe they figure that my feminine name fits her better than it does me. Maybe the combination "is" sound in my name is indistinguishable from the "iz" combination in hers. Maybe my monosyllabic name comes more trippingly off the tongue than Elizabeth does. Or maybe all of our friends have lousy memories and always call each member of a couple by the same name. Whatever the reason, my male ego is grateful that I haven't yet been called Elizabeth.

My first name also causes me some discomfort at Church. For reasons that I don't fully understand, Mormons like calling people by their first name and middle initial: Harold B. Lee, Spencer W. Kimball, Dallin H. Oaks, Bishop FirstName MiddleInitial LastName. You know how it goes. My middle initial is *E.,* and it makes a horrible combination when paired with the shortened form of my first name. Painful memories of my "Chrissy the Sissy" days come flooding back whenever I have to speak in sacrament meeting and the bishop announces that "Brother Chris E. Crowe will now address us."

It's not any better in the temple. I was once asked to give the closing prayer in a meeting in the temple chapel before ward temple night. The temple worker conducting the meeting hadn't met me but had been given my name by our bishop. At the close of our meeting, he stood and announced that "Sister Chris Crowe will now give the benediction."

So maybe you can understand why I think names are so important. Mine has been a minor irritant since my first day of kindergarten, but I've managed to get along in spite of it. Fortunately, my kids—Christy, Jonathan, Carrie, and Joanne— have benefitted from my parents' mistake and will be spared the same kind of name abuse I've had to put up with.

But there is a silver lining to this dark cloud of name abuse: it's helped me relate, in a way, to my Grandfather Crowe. He died long before I was born, and I know precious little about him. But some years ago I discovered that he and I have at least one thing in common, a shared experience of sorts. His first name was Everett.

Friends called him "Eve."

The Ordeal of
Real vs. Ideal

We just finished family home evening, and I couldn't feel worse. I really want to have good home evenings, to use them to grow close to my children, to draw them close to me and to one another, to teach them the gospel. But by the time tonight's lesson ended, all I felt like doing was giving them several swift object lessons on the "laying on of hands."

It went like this: We dispensed with the opening song due to universal apathy and grumpiness. Jonathan muttered a grudging opening prayer. A few minutes into the lesson, Christy sat comatose with her head flopped on the back of the sofa, her eyes rolled up in a disgusted, bored, completely infuriating look that only teenagers can create. Jonathan rolled through a variety of contortions on the loveseat, the most common being one that had his feet where his head should have been and his head on the floor. Carrie and Joanne shared a seat and a running, giggling dialogue punctuated with mutual elbows in ribs, pokes, and tickles throughout the lesson.

I plodded through my tithing lesson with clenched teeth, marveling at how much my own children were acting like my Sunday School class on a really bad day. By the time the lesson was over, I had about as much spirit left in me as an empty whiskey bottle.

And I feel terrible about it, especially when I reflect on our sporadic history of formal home evenings. More often than not, the lesson is quickly discarded and I spend the time dishing out threats and sentences, gradually working my way to my boiling point: I erupt and send them off to bed without home evening treats. Then I go to the kitchen to eat all the treats myself.

That'll teach 'em!

There are multiple guilts eating at me here, making me feel like a pretty pathetic father. First of all, I know we're supposed to have regular home evenings. And I know that they're not supposed to be activities, the one thing we're near perfection on. And I know I'm not supposed to lose my temper. And I know the kids are supposed to enjoy these get-togethers, these lessons. And I know that I should plan meaningful lessons, should involve the kids, should encourage thoughtful discussions about gospel topics. I know all the promises connected with the faithful performance of home evenings. I know all this stuff, and believe it too, but it doesn't help one whit in succeeding at it. No, all this knowledge in the face of all this failure makes me feel pretty depressed.

So do all the calories from my snarfing of the treats.

Part of my discouragement about home evening comes from the huge gulf between how it is and how I wish it were. My fantasy home evening is like a warm and fuzzy Homefront video: *After clearing the dinner table, my son argues amiably with his sisters over who gets to wash the dishes—all want to. He wins. My wife pops a peach pie she had made earlier in the day into the oven. While the aroma of baking pie wafts around us, we happily gather around the piano, where Christy plays Primary songs and we all sing along. I have to use all my authority to end the merry songfest so we can begin our lesson.*

We begin our evening with a hymn, then Jonathan offers a heartfelt invocation, one that neglects no one in our extended family and no continent on earth. We say amen in unison, and I notice several of the kids wiping tears from their eyes. I ask, "Who's got the lesson tonight?" prompting a little good-natured disagreement over who is in charge: all four children have prepared lessons during the past week, and all four want to teach them tonight. My wife settles the conflict by referring to the ornate assignment board that dominates our living room wall: it's Christy's turn.

Christy begins by bearing her testimony, her voice choking with emotion as she expresses love and gratitude for each one of us. Then she delivers a stirring lesson on the importance of obeying parents. She cites ten to fifteen scriptures from memory, reads from the writings of Elder McConkie and four latter-day prophets. All the kids participate joyfully and thoughtfully. All renew their covenants to honor and obey their parents even better than before. Then they leave their chairs to hug and kiss my wife and me. "I love you, Daddy," they each whisper in my ear.

We conclude the lesson with two hymns, Jonathan playing the accompaniment now. Joanne offers a moving benediction, and we go to the kitchen for perfect peach pie straight from the oven. Carrie and Joanne announce they've collaborated on a secret service project for tonight's lesson. They step out to the back porch, retrieve an ice cream maker, and scoop out homemade ice cream for each slice of pie. Before helping themselves, the children make sure Mom and Dad are served first. We then sit around the kitchen table enjoying our dessert and chatting about their activities, Church classes, and straight-A report cards.

By 8:30 Jonathan has already finished washing the dessert dishes, and all the kids are in their bedrooms reading scriptures and writing in their journals before going to bed. Later, when I tuck each one in, they say, "Thanks, Dad, for a really wonderful family home evening!"

Unfortunately, this fantasy home evening exists only in my mind, where it has taken up permanent residence and now niggles at my conscience and temperament each time I endure a real home evening. My fantasy lurks there, making me miserable every time Jonathan yanks the dog's tail instead of joining in the opening song, every time Christy rolls her eyes when her little sisters give a simple answer, every time Carrie and Joanne moan when I announce it's time for family home evening.

The perfect family home evening is not the only fantasy nagging my conscience. Home teaching is right alongside it.

At various times in my life I have been a perfect home teacher. When I was still relatively inexperienced in Church service, I was practically perfect in the letter of the home teaching law: I saw each of my families once a month. When I better understood that home teaching involves more than just showing up every month like a credit card bill, I worked to get to know my assigned families, to help them, to serve them. Though I enjoyed home teaching, I never felt that I was all that good at it. There was always more to do, plenty of room for magnification. Lately my home teaching has degenerated to its lowest point. I'm an inconsistent visitor, more an intrusion than a blessing to my assigned families. And because of my sporadic record, I'm sure I'm a frustration to my high priests group leader.

In my home teaching fantasy, of course, things are different. *I visit each family once a month formally, and informally two or three times more. I regularly take them cookies or treats I've made. I send birthday cards to each family member. I attend their children's concerts, games, and recitals. Not only am I always there when they need me, but they call me first, before the bishop, before my companion, before their own family members, when they need help. I've made a real difference in their lives, and when their kids go on missions, get married, have babies, I will always be the special honored guest at the event.*

When I compare my home teaching performance with my ideal, the Grand Canyon of difference between the two makes me feel pretty lousy, makes me wish sometimes that I could be absolved of the responsibility and its related guilt.

This ongoing and irreconcilable conflict between the ideal and real is one of the hardest things about being a husband, a father, a priesthood holder. I want to be perfect. I want to do things right and well. I want to be a great servant to the Lord, a great husband to my wife, and a great father to my children; when I'm not, it's disappointing, frustrating, depressing.

These negative feelings come in part from my idealism—from my fantasies about how things could be, about how I've been taught and told they should be. But they also result from my own faults. I know how to do all these things right, and I know why, but for some reason knowledge doesn't always lead to performance. Is it because I'm lazy, stupid, or both? Why don't I always do what I'm supposed to do, the way it's supposed to be done?

I'm not overly idealistic, nor am I a Mormon Walter Mitty living out fantasies in my own mind while I ignore the dreary realities of my own abilities. But I am saddled with a great weight, the responsibility to do things well and right for me and for my family. When my feeble efforts fall so short of the perfect mark, it's easy to be disappointed, to wish I could do it better. And maybe that's the block. Maybe the responsibilities of a married Mormon man are so varied, so numerous, so heavy, so daunting, that it's easy to be overwhelmed. And as any swimmer in a riptide knows, when you're trapped in a powerful current, the best thing to do is to stop swimming against it, to let the current sweep you out to sea where you'll be able to swim around it. (Of course, smart swimmers know that it's better to avoid the riptides in the first place.)

So if I were a smart swimmer, a highly effective married Mormon man (if I had mastered the seven habits of highly successful people), I'd avoid getting into the inefficient, nonproductive riptide in the first place. I'd simply do what I'm supposed to do, when I'm supposed to, the way I'm supposed to. That certainly would be healthier, less guilt inducing. Only problem is, I'm by nature inefficient and nonproductive.

Maybe I could go in a different direction. I could alter my fantasies, my ideal versions of how things should be, to allow room for some warts and human foibles. I could, or should, "get real," as my daughter often says. That would give me some room to slop around, to make some mistakes without drowning or giving up. After all, it's not the responsibility that slows me down and discourages me, it's the futility of my puny efforts contrasted with the fantastic ideal I've conjured up.

A little more realism—not in practice, I've got plenty of that—but in principle, that's what I need.

LaVell and Me

I'm sure this will surprise LaVell when it gets out. In the beginning when this all started, I promised I'd keep it just between the two of us until he notched his two hundredth win. Back then he and I both figured that meant forever.

Now it means tomorrow.

January 1972. I was in Utah for the first time in my life, a high school senior on a football recruiting trip to BYU, whose football program had taken more hits than a side of beef in a Rocky movie. BYU's football team was the doormat of the 50s and 60s, a guaranteed victory for Arizona State University, the University of Utah, and any other team lucky enough to land them on their schedule.

On my first night in Provo, head coach Tommy Hudspeth jumped from the sinking ship, and LaVell Edwards, the defensive assistant, was named as his replacement. But even more important to LaVell, the football program, and BYU, that night I made up my mind that I would become a Cougar.

When I reported for fall practice, I met with LaVell—Lav, he asked me to call him—to talk about how we could turn the program around. He was desperate to do something, to make a change, to keep his job, and when I looked at the pathetic experience he had—coach at Granite High School, defensive coach of a bunch of lousy BYU teams—I had pity on him and agreed to do what I could to help. We decided, however, to keep my consultations secret. After all, I had my own career to worry about, and quite frankly I didn't really believe we'd be able to make a whole lot of progress. So I promised him that if we did manage to squeeze some success out of the BYU football rock, he could have all the credit.

Our first strategy meeting was a disaster. As a former defensive coach, he had a Civil War attitude about football: "The best offense is a good defense," and "Wars are won in the trenches." Without even consulting me, he had decided to emphasize defense.

"Big mistake. I'd pass."

Lav pushed his cap back on his head and gave me that famous hang-dog look. "You'd what?"

"Throw the ball, air it out, bomb the defensive backs, score points."

"But you win games with *defense*."

"Sorry, Lav, but it looks to me like around here you've been *losing* games with defense."

He scowled thoughtfully.

"C'mon, Coach, this is the 70s, for pete's sake. Throw the ball!"

He squirmed and recited the conservative coach's mantra: "But when you throw the ball, only four things can happen, and three of them are bad."

"Well, then, I guess I can't help you."

"No, wait. I'll listen, I'll listen, but you've got to give me some time to get used to all this."

"Okay. Look at it this way: the air war saved England and crushed Japan, right? Modern football is no longer a game of inches battled out in the trenches. The forward pass is the answer, the wave of the future."

His scowl softened.

"Tell you what: you got a kid, Pete van Valkenburg, looks like a decent running back. Why not give him the ball twenty to thirty times a game this season and let him carry the team? The way I see it, he might even end up leading the nation in rushing. Make this your last year of the ground game, and then start training your air corps for next season."

His lopsided grin told me I had him convinced. We shook hands on it.

"And, Lav," I said on my way out the door, "that kid Paul Howard? Move him from defense to offense. He's got a future on the offensive line."

So that 1972 season, our first year at the helm, went better than anyone's expectations. Lav couldn't even believe we ended up 7-4, and he couldn't thank me enough. "No problem, Lav. Just give me all the credit about 193 wins from now." We both laughed and laughed.

That winter I pushed him hard to recruit a quarterback with an arm, someone who could step in and play. But despite my tutoring, he slipped back into his old pattern: recruiting linebackers and monstrous defensive linemen. I dropped by his office one afternoon to straighten him out.

"You don't need eight more defensive tackles. This junior college kid in California, Gary Sheide? I say you take a gamble on him. Sure he's damaged goods, but the kid's got a good arm. Sign him and let him throw the ball."

Now it doesn't bother or surprise me at all that Lav's forgotten that conversation and that when he tells the history of Quarterback U, he leaves my role out of it. As far as the public knew, I was only a puny and obscure second-string offensive tackle. He was the head coach—the figurehead coach, at least—and I did agree to let him have the glory.

Sheide did all right. Lav started seeing the light about the passing game, so it wasn't all that hard to talk him into signing a basketball player–quarterback, Gifford Neilson, the next year.

"Are you sure, Chris? A basketball player? Will he last a season?"

"Trust me on this, Lav. The kid'll be fine."

You'd have thought he would have learned after Giff, but old defensive coaches can't learn new tricks in a day. After my senior season, when I told him to sign Marc Wilson, he still balked.

"Too skinny. He'll never make it here."

I just shook my head and sighed. "Lav, I'm losing patience with you. Sign the kid; play him. You'll see."

My last semester at BYU was hectic. I was trying to graduate and find a job, but try as I might, I couldn't get away from Lav's calls and messages, pleading with me to have one more strategy session with him before I left for good.

Success hadn't changed him much, but it certainly had changed his office and his wardrobe. The old nylon coaching shirt and baggy sweatpants were gone, replaced by a tony polo shirt and golf slacks, and his office had been remodeled and enlarged to hold his executive walnut desk and monstrously gaudy bowl game trophies.

"Sit down, Chris." He pulled out a chair in front of his desk. "Now, I just want your input on a couple things here, you know, get things squared away before you leave." He slid his quarterback recruit list across the desk tentatively.

"Lav," I sighed, "you've got to start making these decisions on your own. I won't always be here to do this for you."

"I know, I know. This is the last time, I promise. But we've got a flock of promising young QB recruits. California, Texas, Arizona . . ."

"Take the McMahon kid from Roy."

"You're kidding. He's not LDS."

"Sure he's got some rough edges, but he's a winner. The kid can throw. Just don't bring him along too soon or you'll have a real nasty situation between him and Wilson. Keep McMahon on ice till Marc's graduated."

Lav thanked me profusely, said I'd done more than anyone to save the football program, to turn them into a winner. He went on and on, waxing pretty sentimental, as only Lav can, so I cut him short before he started gushing tears of gratitude.

"Look, Lav, it's been fun. To tell you the truth, when we started on this I didn't think we had a prayer to pull it off. But I've enjoyed playing football here, talking with you, giving you what help I can." I shook his hand. He pulled me into a humble but awkward embrace of thanks. When we separated, tears rimmed his eyelids.

"C'mon, get a hold of yourself. You'll be fine without me."

That hang-dog look again. Man, he made me feel so *guilty,* like I was deserting him or something.

"Okay, here's a final bit of advice, Coach: Cougar Stadium needs to be remodeled. Double its capacity and you'll have a legitimate nationally recognized football program."

He laughed. "You've got to be kidding. We can barely fill it up now. If we go to sixty-five thousand, we'll never sell it out.

And besides, who's going to pay for it? The university sure won't."

"No problem. You've got an increasingly rabid Cougar Club. Let them head up the stadium cause; use donated funds only. It'll be great PR. And I promise you, Lav, if you build it, they will come."

I have to admit, Lav did all right after I left. He found Robbie Bosco all by himself, and managed to win the national championship in 1984 calling me only every other week instead of every week for advice. He continued to call periodically, "Just seeing how you are," he'd say, when I knew he really wanted my input on this or that. But I didn't begrudge him my advice over the years. Heaven knows, he needed it, and he's had the good sense to put it to good use. I'm not trying to brag, but he wouldn't have had the success he's had without me in the background, nudging him when he needed it. I turned him on to a Connecticut quarterback, Steve Young, a while back. "But we don't recruit in *Connecticut*," he said. "Trust me," I said. "Sign him," I said. And to Lav's credit, he did. Getting him to sign Ty Detmer was even harder. "He's short, he's skinny, and he's not LDS. I'm not close-minded, Chris, you know that, but after Jim McMahon, I'm not sure I can take any more nonmember QBs." I sighed patiently, remembering that he was, after all, still a little insecure without me right there to call the shots for him. "This kid," I said, "will be different—and better. I guarantee it." And the rest, as they say, is history.

LaVell and me have created a pretty decent football program at BYU, even if I do say so myself (which, I guess, I have to, since *he's* not saying anything). He had a down year last year, the worst since we started in Provo, and not coincidentally, the first year I left him entirely on his own. But now I live in Utah Valley myself and work in BYU's English department, close enough for Lav to come by often to chat about "his" team. And like I said, I don't mind helping him out, really haven't minded it at all, but now that we're approaching number 200, well, it's time for the real history of BYU's football success to be known.

The Sins of the Fathers
and Vice Versa

My dad had chronic wanderlust. I realized that long before I even knew there was a word to describe it. I was born in Danville, Illinois; when I was two or three years old we moved to Normal, Illinois. A couple years later we moved to Bloomington, Illinois, where I started school. Four years later our wanderings in the wilderness really began: Santa Fe, then Las Cruces, New Mexico; Carmichael, then Dublin, California. Tempe, Arizona, became a longer stopover, one where I started and finished high school, joined the Church, and joined my wife. My parents went on from there to Oklahoma, Mississippi, Louisiana, and various points in Texas, where they have settled down for what looks like good.

Moving around so much wasn't as bad as it may seem. Our family was rock-solid and more tightly knit than Lycra, so moving didn't faze us. But after a three-different-schools-in-two-states year (sixth grade), I began to wonder if it wouldn't be better to stay put for a while, to dig in and live in one place long enough to memorize its zip code. That's also probably about the time pubescent hormones and Oedipus-Hamlet stuff started working on me. My dad, I began to realize, had faults, wanderlust being a major one. And not only did I have an eye keen enough to discern his every flaw, I also had all the answers; too bad he didn't have the good sense to ask me.

It was then that I knew I'd be smarter than my dad, and I started making statements like, "When I'm a (fill in the blank: parent, husband, businessman, adult), I'll *never* (fill in the blank with the latest faux pas committed by my father). Of course, I knew better than to trumpet such mutinous stuff around my parents. I kept it bottled up in my rebellious little head, and the more it bounced around in there, the more sense it made to me, the more it convinced me that I really knew what was what about what.

Of course, it's one of life's great and inevitable ironies that what goes around comes around. When you're a kid, at least when I was a kid, I smugly nitpicked every little mote from my dad's eye, all the while saying, "When *I'm* in that position, I will *never* . . ."

This kind of know-it-all-ism didn't end after I grew up. Before I had children of my own, the obnoxious behavior of other people's kids annoyed me to no end, and I continued my myopic predictions with all the smugness of my childhood: "*My* kids will never do that." The double curse of making such proclamations (and whether it's an Oedipal curse, a Hamletian curse, or just plain divine retribution really doesn't matter) is that I have been wrong, doubly dead wrong, on both counts.

The light dawned dimly, but it didn't take long before it grew into a megawatt searchlight exposing my errors. Soon after I was married I discovered myself speaking and acting in many ways *exactly like Dad!* And that was only the beginning of my excruciating epiphany. Once our kids started coming along, I'd catch myself letting a howling one remain in sacrament meeting. I let them crawl on dirty sidewalks, pull things off store shelves, poke other little kids, play outside wearing crusty-snotty noses and grimy t-shirts. *My* kids, my own children, were *regularly* doing things that I had publicly proclaimed they'd *never* do! These sins, these vain predictions—all these and more, many more—have been answered on my head.

Ouch. Double ouch.

I think I now understand why I was so far off predicting my children's behavior: I was stupid, idealistic, and inexperienced. I had no idea how wearing children could be; I didn't know that even as infants they'd have willful minds of their own. And my brain had blotted out any recollection of my own early childhood behavior. But the main reason is that, in my pre-parenthood days, I honestly believed that kids' behavior was a direct result of parenting, that kids were lumps of clay ready to be molded by their parents. Wise and good parents molded kids who wouldn't scream in sacrament meetings, who wouldn't jam Cheerios into other kids' ears, who wouldn't toddle around in public with snotty noses and loaded diapers.

And, of course, my pre-parental idealism blinded me to the realities of rearing children. Such idealism is necessary because without it, many of us would never have the courage to *have* children in the first place. So I went smugly down the pre-parenthood path condemning the lousy parents around me, while believing—no, knowing—that things would be different with me and my kids. I now know that even though parents do have a lot of influence on kids' behavior, they don't have total control over it. I also know that many of the things that annoyed me in other kids didn't faze me in my own. Depending on what I was doing at the time, I had incredible tolerance for all kinds of obnoxious behavior, odors, and sounds from my own children.

My penance has been just but painful. I now endure, in silence, the critical stares, murmurs, and occasional comments of childless people who witness my children's public imperfections.

There's a saying in Japanese: *"Kaeru no ko wa kaeru desu,"* the child of a frog is a frog. I hadn't heard this when I was young; if I had, I wouldn't have believed it anyway. But now that I'm a husband and father myself, I recognize the inevitability of genetics. Despite my childhood wisdom and predictions to the contrary, it's only natural that I'd have many of my father's characteristics: I am my father's son.

For example, the wanderlust.

After I graduated from BYU I spent a semester teaching in Ogden before we moved back to Arizona: home. Permanent home. I prided myself on my lack of mobility, my unCroweish stability. Nobody had to tear out address book pages on our account. My wife and I lived in the same house, I worked the same job, for ten years. But then things began to change.

First we moved to Japan for a year. Then back to Arizona. Then to Japan again (two different apartments), this time for almost three years. Then to Hawaii, four years at two different addresses. Then to Utah, Springville for a year and finally Provo—a place, a house, a home we are predicting will be the end of the trail. This is the place where we plan to sink the taproot, to see our kids through adolescence, to grow old and hoary.

Of course, we've said that five or six times before.

Until a few nights ago I hadn't considered myself adventuresome or nomadic or any more mobile than the next guy. I had always pictured my little family as a stable bunch that didn't take change well and liked the status quo. I believed this despite the trail of forwarding addresses we've left behind us in the last decade. Anyway, we were at a block party getting to know our new neighbors, and the host, who had heard me in priesthood meeting describe the wandering path that led us to Provo, said, "You guys really get around, don't you?" and went on to marvel at how mobile and footloose we were.

Mobile? Footloose? Me? No, I hate moving. I would never subject my kids to the nomadic life I had endured.

That's when the arc-light of truth and reality hit me full in the face. I have been pretty nomadic; I have dragged my kids from place to place. Just like Dad. But now that I have the perspective Dad must have had when we moved around, it seems so much more *reasonable* to me. You follow opportunities; you move your family to places where they can thrive; as a father, you do what you think is best for the family. Dad must have had the same reasons, the same motivations for every move we made.

That epiphany made me wonder about how much of Dad is in me. Of course, I've taken on many of his good traits: reading, discipline, a willingness to work, taking pleasure in other people, loving my family, and many more. But self-examination reveals that I've also taken on some of the very characteristics of his that I used to forswear. And these traits annoy my children just as much as they used to annoy me.

I tease my kids and their friends too much and too relentlessly. I run jokes into the ground. I deliver long and serious sermons over trivial matters. I overdose advice, even when it's not wanted. I'm opinionated, even when I claim not to be. My temper is sometimes short and erratic. I eat too much. I do things that embarrass my children in public.

I still have a vivid memory of these weaknesses in Dad, and just as vivid is my recollection of the many times I swore that these weaknesses would never be mine. But now, as my kids will testify, they are.

It is embarrassing and humbling and eye opening. And I wonder what I can do about it. Fortunately for me, these genetic peccadilloes are not all that serious; mostly they just annoy my children. It could be worse: a cycle of abuse, alcoholism, or some other social disorder. Now that these flaws have manifested themselves in me, I want to work on getting rid of them before they infect my own children. But it may be too late. Already I've seen the fruits of my errors: my son is a merciless tease; my fifteen-year-old daughter often proclaims that when *she's* a parent, *she'll* never do the annoying, restrictive, dumb, old-fashioned things I do.

No, she says, she'll be different.

I just smile and hope she will be.